Step by Step Art 5

Christmas in the Classroom

Published by
Topical Resources

Introduction

This book aims to provide a simple easy to follow approach to Christmas displays and decorations in school. It hopes to stimulate teachers and provide them with fail-safe activities resulting, hopefully, in a satisfying and frequently stunning outcome!.

The activities are in themes for easy access but don't necessarily have to be interpreted as such. Themes can however have considerable impact if they are followed, for example down a corridor or around a resource area. Colour schemes too can enhance displays and unite a range of different activities and invite the eye to appreciate them as a whole rather than a number of conflicting and clashing arrangements, each one successful in its own right but not in harmony with the one adjacent to it. Try a colour scheme to link the range of work in a hall-area, along a corridor or even around a classroom! Suggestions for colour schemes are to be found at the beginning of the book.

Each example in the book is illustrated for easy understanding as well as being described in detail. The materials needed for each activity are listed and the "What to do" section outlines the instructions the teacher needs to give when working through an activity with the children. Several of the techniques, e.g. marbling or paint-brush skills could be explored before the Christmas season, the results saved and later converted and used as an ingredient in the making of decorations for Christmas displays. It doesn't all need to happen in a frenzy during the last couple of weeks amid parties and productions!

The examples are not divided into Key Stages. Choice of activity is left to the discretion of teachers, their knowledge of the children in their class and their own confidence in their approach to Art and Design activities. Most of the examples are appropriate to any Key Stage including the Foundation Stage, though some could and might need to be elaborated or simplified accordingly.

I hope you will enjoy trying the ideas in this book and that you and the children involved will be pleased and satisfied with the end results. Good luck, and may I wish you many happy and successful Christmases in school!

Dianne Williams

The publishers have endeavoured to trace the copyright holders of all the images used in this publication. If we have unwittingly infringed copyright, we sincerely apologise and will we pleased, on being satisfied as to the owner's title, to pay an appropriate fee as if we had been able to obtain prior permission.

Step by Step Art Books 1-5 are available from all good Educational Bookshops and by mail order from:

Topical Resources, P.O. Box 329, Broughton, Preston, Lancashire. PR3 5LT

Topical Resources publishes a range of Educational Materials for use in Primary Schools and Pre-School Nurseries and Playgroups.

For the latest catalogue:
Tel 01772 863158 Fax 01772 866153
e-mail: sales@topical-resources.co.uk
Visit our Website at:
www.topical-resources.co.uk

Copyright © 2001 Dianne Williams

Printed in Great Britain for "Topical Resources", Publishers of Educational Materials, P.O. Box 329, Broughton, Preston, Lancashire PR3 5LT by T.Snape & Company Limited, Boltons Court, Preston Lancashire.

Typeset by Paul Sealey Illustration & Design, 3 Wentworth Drive, Thornton, Lancashire.

First Published September 2001.
ISBN 1 872977 60 X

Contents

COLOUR SCHEMES

The simplest way to unify a school at christmas is with colour. A range of different work on individual boards e.g. down a corridor, around the hall or resource area will have maximum impact if all the boards are backed with the same or similar colours. Try a colour scheme for all the boards in your own classroom initially to convince yourself - and others - of the impact limited and related colour can have.

Suggested Colour Schemes :-

Red, yellow, orange and gold - this is a range of rich glowing colours.

Blue, pink, purple and silver - a colder range of colours that work well together.

Blue, grey, white and silver - a cool range suggesting a wintry theme.

Purple, pink, burgundy and silver - another rich group of strong colours.

Red, green, white, and gold - a traditional Christmas colour scheme.

Black, silver, red, grey and white - a dramatic colour scheme, ideal for silhouettes.

Brown, yellow, white and gold - a warm, mellow group of colours.

Green, blue, white and silver - these create a fresh, crisp feel.

Yellow, blue, white, gold and silver - a contrasting and striking group of colours.

The combinations of colour suggested here are by no means the only ones to try. When considering a colour scheme do not try to involve too many colours, three or four at the most work best. All schemes will benefit from and work well with some neutrals e.g. grey, black and white. Sometimes if only a few colours are chosen the scheme might need a lift, in this case it might benefit from several shades of the same colour for extra interest rather than an additional colour. If the school decides on a Christmas theme e.g. Snow and Ice or Stained Glass Windows, the colour scheme will need to match and be appropriate to that theme. Blues and silvers are not ideal for robins and Santa Claus!

Once the colour scheme has been decided on, plenty of extra paper in that particular range of colours will need to be ordered well in advance so that each member of staff gets their fair share and the stock cupboard is not completely depleted. Sheets of paper, rather than rolls, can prove more economical and easier to handle especially if there are light switches and such to cut round.

Giving each member of staff a sample swatch of the colours in the chosen colour scheme will remind them of the colours for their displays - and to use with the children. If for example, they are doing a design in stitching for a calendar, it will be a useful prompt as they plan and gather appropriate ideas, in readiness, beforehand. Also it will provide the starting point for collections of their own. E.g. fancy foil, wrapping paper, doilies etc. and give opportunities for them to discuss with the class the contribution they could look out for and add to the resources.

Red, yellow, orange and gold
- this is a range of rich glowing colours.

Blue, pink, purple and silver
- a colder range of colours that work well together.

Blue, grey, white and silver
- a cool range suggesting a wintry theme

Purple, pink burgundy and silver
- another rich group of strong colours.

Red, green, white, and gold
- a traditional Christmas colour scheme.

Black, silver, red, grey and white
- a dramatic colour scheme ideal for silhouettes.

Brown, yellow, white and gold
- a warm, mellow group of colours.

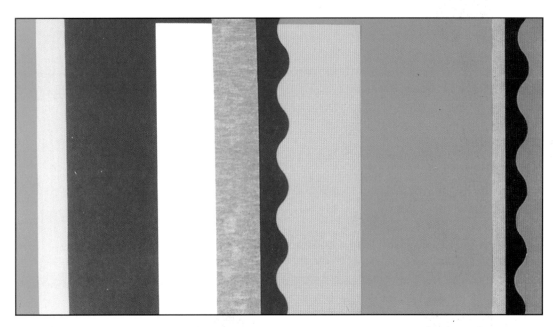

Green, blue, white and silver
- these create a fresh, crisp feel.

Yellow, blue, white, gold and silver
- a contrasting and striking group of colours.

7

1. Stars and Swirls

Materials Needed: Red, yellow and white ready mixed paint, pieces of card to use as mixing palettes, paint brushes, oil pastel crayons, pre-cut gold foil stars and circles, glue, art straws, white paper (80 gsm).

What to Do: Allow experimentation and practice in making swirling movements and patterns with an unloaded paint-brush on paper before providing blobs of the different paints on a palette to be used for the same. Encourage the use of pure colour for some of the swirls and colour mixing for others. The swirls need to touch and eventually fill the page. Allow the paint to dry before over drawing with red and orange oil pastel to outline and emphasise the swirls. Arrange a few of the pre-cut gold stars and circles at random on the pattern. Cut some small lengths from the art straws and stick them to radiate from the stars. This could be a large scale collaborative piece of work or individual pieces unmounted and displayed together as a block.

2. Marbled Patchwork with a Star

Materials Needed: White paper (80 gsm), marbling inks, a shallow tray, a single hole punch, scissors, glue, pre-cut silver star.

What to Do: Half fill the shallow tray with water and drip a few drops of two or three colours of marbling ink on to the surface of the water. Swirl the inks around with an old fork or comb to mix and mingle the colours and break up any blobs. Check that the paper is the right size for the tray before laying it briefly on the surface of the inky water. Lift the paper off to reveal the print and allow it to dry. Take a second print from the same tray (it will be fainter than the first) before adding more ink and taking another print. When the marbling is dry, cut it into a series of squares and arrange them as a patchwork on a piece of white paper. They need to fill the paper with only small gaps between the squares. Use the single hole punch to punch circles from any left over marbling. Use the pre - cut silver star as a guide to cut a slightly larger star out of white paper. Glue this down first in one corner of the patchwork and place the silver one on top. Add decoration around the silver star with the punched out circles.

3. Marbled Stars

Materials Needed: Marbling inks and a shallow tray as before, white paper (80 gsm), blue and pink ready mixed paint, pieces of card to use as a palette, cotton wool buds for printing, art straws, single hole punch, scissors and glue.

What to Do: Produce marbled paper as described previously and allow it to dry. Draw round the star template several times on the back of the marbled paper. Cut the stars out and stick them on a piece of white paper. Leave gaps between the stars. Put some ready mixed paint on a piece of card and with a cotton wool bud print lines of dots radiating from each star. Use one colour only for each star. Add some short strips of art straws and punched circles to decorate some of the stars.

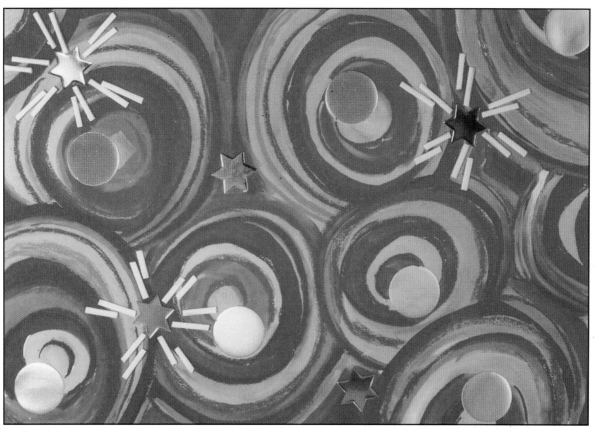

1. Stars and Swirls

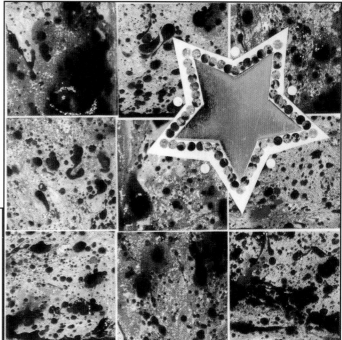

2. Marbled Patchwork with a Star

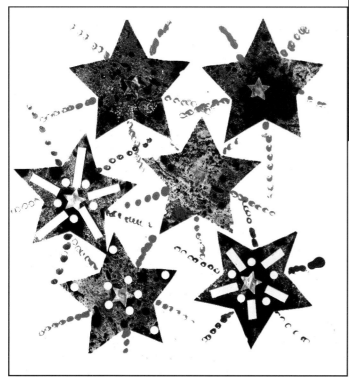

3. Marbled Stars

4. Smudged Chalk Circle and Star

Materials Needed: Chalk or chalk pastel in blue, white, pink and purple, paper towels cut into squares for blending colour, grey sugar paper, and pre-cut silver stars.

What to Do: Start in the centre of the grey paper with white chalk pastel and draw and fill a circular shape. Choose a pastel of another colour, use it on its side and colour a thick ring round the circle. Use a paper towel to smudge and blend the edges of the circle and the ring together. Choose a further colour and add and blend another ring. Continue in the same way until a large multi ringed smudged circle has been created. Stick a pre- cut silver star in the centre of the white circle. A collection of these en masse would make a stunning display. Fix the pastel by spraying it with hair spray before putting the work on display.

5. Chalk Star Outlines

Materials Needed: Dark coloured paper as a background, purple, blue and white chalks or chalk pastels and a star template.

What to Do: Place the star template in the middle of the dark coloured background paper and draw round it with a white chalk. Remove the template but use the shape it has left as the basis for a design of thick and thin lines, star outlines, spiky shapes and filled in shapes using all the colours of the chalks. Continue the design to the edge of the paper - if it varies and is irregular it will be more interesting. Fix the design with a squirt of hair spray to prevent it smudging.

6. Colour Family Collage with a Star

Materials Needed: Small squares of white paper as a background, glue, scissors, pre-cut foil stars, assorted papers in different shades for each colour family.

What to Do: Decide on a colour family to be used and select a range of papers in different shades of that colour. Cut the papers into small rectangular or square shapes and glue them close together to cover the white background paper. Glue a foil star in the middle of the finished collage.

7. Drip Grid Paper Star Collage

Materials Needed: Plain Poster paper (in this case blue) white ready mixed paint, paint-brushes, pieces of card as paint palettes, glue, scissors, silver foil, white background paper, and pre-cut foil stars.

What to Do: Prior to assembling the collage, drip grid paper needs to be produced. This is done by fastening the poster paper to an easel or a tilted piece of card, loading a paint brush with runny paint i.e. ready mixed paint plus plenty of water, dragging it across the top of the poster paper and allowing the paint to drip and run down it in an irregular way. Several brush loads may be necessary for a strong grid pattern. Allow the poster paper to dry before cutting it into strips. Stick a foil star in the middle of a piece of white background paper and use the drip grid strips and strips of silver foil to create a collage around it. Mount the finished collage on poster paper that matches the coloured paper behind the drip grid.

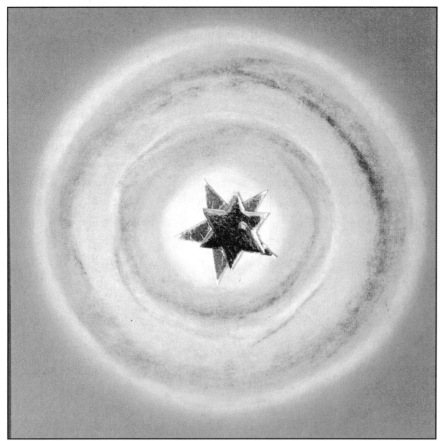

4. Smudged Chalk Circle and Star

5. Chalk Star Outlines

6. Colour Family Collage with a Star

7. Drip Grid Paper Star Collage

8. Stars and Doilies Design

Materials Needed: Small white doilies, white paper as a background, blue, silver red and white ready mixed paint, sponge rollers, pieces of card to use as mixing palettes, newspaper, glue and pre- cut star shapes.

What to Do: Place some of the white doilies on pieces of newspaper and with a sponge roller cover the surface of each with either silver or purple paint. Lay more white doilies and star shapes on the white background paper and with a sponge roller cover the surface of these with blue paint. Cover the white background paper in the same colour with the roller as well. Remove the stars and doilies to reveal white shapes underneath. Arrange and glue the purple and silver doilies on this patterned background and add some of the blue doilies you previously removed as well.

9. Black and White Stars

Materials Needed: White paper, pieces of black paper as a background, glue, scissors, star templates to draw round, pencils, black felt pens, red sticky or poster paper and silver foil.

What to Do: Use the star template to draw round on the white paper. Cut the star shape out carefully and with a black felt pen add patterns to decorate the star. Think of where the different patterns could go - around the edge, in the centre, radiating from the centre etc. When this star has been decorated use the template to draw round and cut out further stars. Decorate each one with several different patterns. Cut some smaller stars out of red paper, fold them in half and cut shapes out along the fold to create a pattern. Scatter the white patterned stars and the red stars across a piece of black background paper before gluing them down. Cut some strips of silver foil to radiate from the stars.

10. Stars with Cut Out Patterns

Materials Needed: Brightly coloured paper as a background (in this case orange), glue, scissors, black paper, star template, pencils and a gold glitter glue pen.

What to Do: Place the star template on a piece of black paper, draw round it and cut it out carefully. Fold each arm of the star in turn and cut out similar shapes along each fold - leave plenty of the fold uncut so that the star shape remains complete. Open the star shape up to reveal the pattern. Draw round and cut out several further stars. Fold and cut patterns in each one. Try to vary the shapes cut out each time to produce different patterns. Stick the stars on to the brightly coloured background paper and add further decoration to them using the gold glitter glue pen. Cut wavy strips of black paper to divide up the design.

11. Wool Winding Stars

Materials Needed: Small paper plates, scissors, double sided sellotape, purple/blue yarn, gold foil, cerise foil, purple poster paper, a glitter glue pen and squares of white paper as the background.

What to Do: Cut slits around the edge of the paper plate and stick a strip of double sided sellotape on the back of it. Press the end of the yarn on to the double sided tape. Randomly wrap the yarn through the slits across the plate in different directions, to form an irregular web pattern. Finish off the yarn by pressing it on the double sided tape. Decorate the wrapped web with blobs of glitter glue or sequins. To display, stick a circle of purple poster paper in the middle of a square of white paper and stick the wrapped plate in the centre of it. Decorate the edge of the poster paper circle with different sized circles of gold and cerise foil and blobs of glitter glue.

8. Stars and Doilies Design

11. Wool Winding Stars

9. Black and White Stars

10. Stars with
Cut Out Patterns

12. Corrugated Paper Star Design

Materials Needed: Squares of white paper or thin card as a background, glue, scissors, strips of corrugated paper and pieces of corrugated paper

What to Do: Cut a small square of corrugated paper and stick it in the middle of the background paper. Cut four small triangles of corrugated paper to radiate from it- the apex of each pointing at the centre square - fill the gaps between them with strips and narrow pieces of corrugated paper. Add three strips of decreasing size at the base of each triangle. Cut some long strips to surround the design so far and create a diamond shape. Add a large triangle of corrugated paper to each edge of the diamond - making a square - and outline the square with long strips of corrugated paper. For display, mount the work on a dark coloured background surrounded by a paler colour.

13. Textile Hanging with Stars

Materials Needed: A strip of cane or dowelling, yarns, ribbons, crepe paper strips in different shades of blue and white, plus foil or sequin-strip cut into narrow strips.

What to Do: Create a series of thin lengths of knitting, plaiting, twisting and finger knitting to hang from and loop across the dowelling. They need to be in a variety of different lengths for interest. Add further strips of crepe paper, ribbon and sequin strip in the same colours as the wool. Decorate the hanging further with bows and pom poms made from wool and silver foil circles and stars. This piece will involve a group or even the whole class combining a variety of individual contributions to create the hanging. To display, hang the completed work above a silhouette of chimney pots.

14. Stars Through a Window

Materials Needed: Large sheets of blue and white paper, sponge rollers, red, blue, silver and white ready mixed paint, silver foil stars, cotton wool buds for printing, glue, scissors, paint-brushes, and pieces of card to use as paint palettes.

What to Do: Take a large sheet of white paper and cover it with blue paint using a sponge roller. Over roll this with some silver paint. Stick on some silver foil stars and with a cotton wool bud and blue and white paint, print some curving rows of dots around the stars. Mount this piece of work on a large piece of blue paper. Fold a large sheet of white paper and cut out the shape of a window with large empty panes. Stick this window frame over the starry background. Paint a further piece of white paper with stripes of red, pink and blue. When this paper is dry, cut it into strips and glue the strips either side of the window frame, as curtains. Cut and concertina fold a wider strip as a pelmet across the top of the curtains. If several children were to produce similar work they might be encouraged to vary the window shapes and the colours and patterns on the curtains. Poetry regarding night skies or wishes would work well in a display of this nature.

15. Foil and Corrugated Paper Stars

Materials Needed: Squares of card as a background, strips and pieces of brown corrugated paper, gold and copper foil, a star template, glue, scissors, pencils and a single hole punch.

What to Do: Choose a piece of card as a background and cover it with foil or corrugated paper. Add strips of corrugated paper around the edge of the square. Draw and cut out a star shape for the centre of the square, punch a pattern of holes in it with the single hole punch before sticking it down. Add further strips of both colours of foils to the design, some could be plain whilst others have a punched pattern in them. Sprinkle the punched out dots around the design.

12. Corrugated Paper Star Design

14. Stars Through a Window

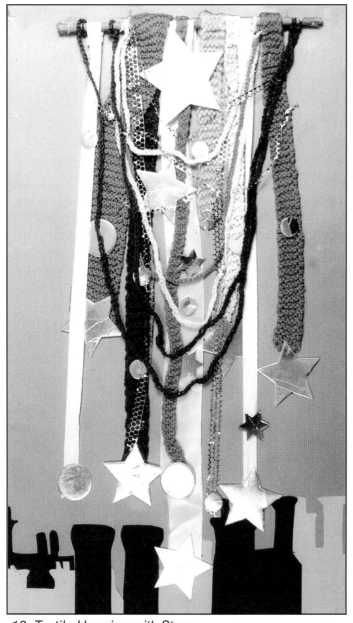

13. Textile Hanging with Stars

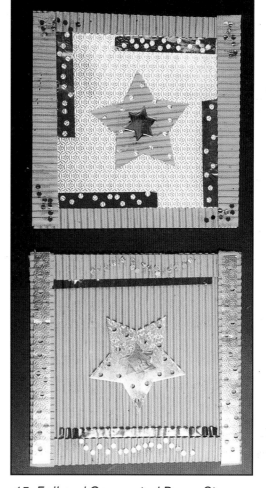

15. Foil and Corrugated Paper Stars

CANDLES

1. Massed Candles and Swirls

Materials Needed: Thin strips of white paper, black sugar paper as a background, red, gold and copper foil, scissors, glue, pencils, cotton wool buds for printing, white, red and yellow ready mixed paint, sponge rollers, pieces of card as mixing palettes and black felt-tip pens.

What to Do: Put several blobs of red, yellow and white ready mixed paint on a card palette and roll the sponge roller across the blobs to pick up an irregular mix of colours and to blend and mix some of the blobs together. Put the loaded roller on to the black paper, press it down gently and swirl it round to create a circle of colour. Add further circles in the same way, returning when necessary to the palette for more mixtures of paint - include some blobs of single colours as well. Try swirls on top of swirls for rich colour. Build up a mass of overlapping swirls across the whole of the black paper. Cut the strips of white paper into different lengths and stick them at different levels among the swirls. Draw and cut some circles of different sizes out of foil and arrange them as flames. Make some of the circles solid and others hollow - to do this fold a circle in half and cut out an inner half circle following the edge of the folded circle. Use cotton wool buds and paint to print dots following and outlining the edges of the circles. Add a thin black line to each candle with a felt-tip pen, as the wick.

2. Cut Patterned Candles and Swirls

Materials Needed: Strips of white paper, squares of black paper as a background, red and gold foil, red, white and yellow ready mixed paint, glue, scissors, cotton wool buds for printing, black felt-tip pens, sponge rollers and pieces of card to use as mixing palettes.

What to Do: Put blobs of paint on a card palette and as in the previous example, mix and blend the colours with a sponge roller before creating one or several swirls on the black paper. This time, limit the swirls to the top and centre of the paper. Cut the white strips into different lengths, fold each strip in half lengthwise and cut shapes along the edge and along the fold - remember to leave parts of the fold uncut to hold the strip together. Open the cut strip to reveal the pattern and stick it (or them) on and downwards from the swirls. Use paint and a cotton wool bud to print dots around the swirls and/or radiating from the wick. Draw the wick with a black felt-tip pen. Add a border with strips and circles of foil.

1. Massed Candles and Swirls

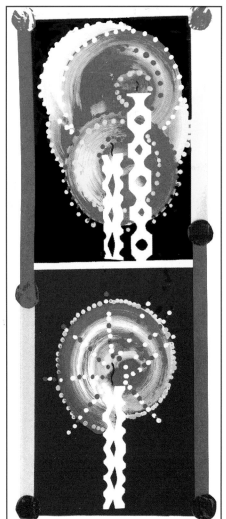

2. Cut Patterned
Candles and
Swirls

17

3. Red Candles with Patterned Flames

Materials Needed: Circles of white paper as the flames, wide strips of red paper as candles, scissors, glue, black felt-tip pens, small pieces of yellow and white paper, thin strips of card, red, yellow, black and white ready mixed paint, pieces of card to use as mixing palettes, and black paper to use as a background.

What to Do: Choose a circle of white paper and in the centre of it put a blob of one colour of paint. Explore swirling or dragging this paint outwards using fingers before putting some blobs of another colour around the edge of the first and making a further finger pattern. Allow the colours to mix and overlap slightly. Add a further colour to the outside of the ring and make a different pattern again. Use the card strips to drag lines in the wet paint or to print lines on the paint once it is dry. Choose further white circles and work in a similar way. Try different patterns and different sequences of colour on each one. Mount the circles on yellow paper when they are dry and cut a larger circle around them to outline each one. Arrange the circles at different levels across the black background, allowing room for a red strip candle under each one. Cut flames of different sizes for each candle out of both yellow and white paper and stick them one on top of the other at the top of each candle. Draw in the wicks with a black felt-tip pen.

4. Cut Strip Decorated Candle

Materials Needed: Wide strips of black paper cut into candle shapes, small pieces of gold foil and red paper, narrow strips of red, yellow, black and orange paper and gold foil, rectangles of gold paper as a background, black felt-tip pens, glue and scissors.

What to Do: Choose several strips of the different coloured papers and experiment with changing one or both edges of each (top and bottom) in different ways i.e. by cutting out rows of different shapes. Lay the strips across a black candle shape with gaps between them. Stick them down and trim off any bits that overhang the edge of the candle - (do this by turning the candle over and cutting carefully along the candle edge.) Mount the candle on the gold background paper, cut two circles of different sizes out of the gold foil and red paper to go on top of each other at the top of the candle. Draw in the wick with a felt-tip pen and cut some thin strips of black to radiate from it. For display use a background paper that matches one of the colours used for the strips.

5. White Candle on a Circle of Strips

Materials Needed: Circles of grey sugar paper, glue, scissors, pieces of white paper, blue, pink and purple paper in a variety of shades cut into strips of different widths and a black felt-tip pen.

What to Do: Choose a grey sugar paper circle and across it arrange strips of the different coloured papers in rows that touch each other. Aim for a varied mix of colours and widths. Stick the strips down and trim off any overlap by turning the circle over and cutting carefully along its outside edge. Cut out the shape of a candle and its flame from white paper and stick in the middle of the circle. Draw the wick in with a felt-tip pen.

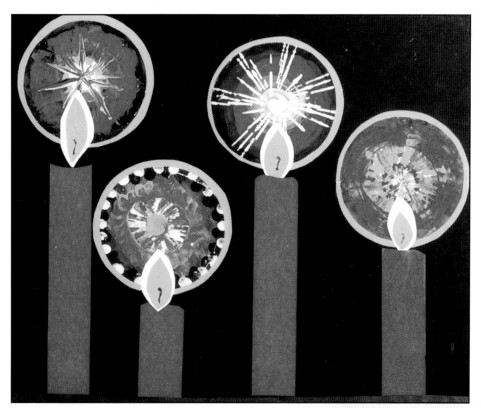

3. Red Candles with Patterned Flames

5. White Candle on a Circle of Strips

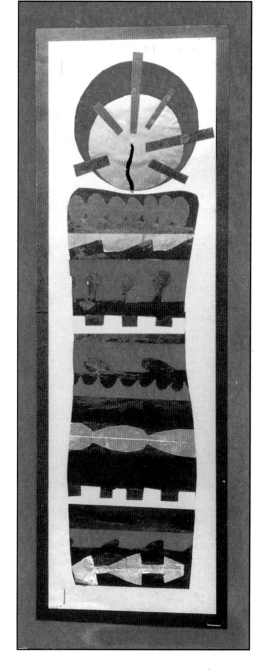

*4. Cut Strip
Decorated
Candle*

6. Patch Work Candle

Materials Needed: A3 white paper, red, blue and white ready mixed paint, paint-brushes, pieces of card to use as mixing palettes, rectangles of blue paper as a background, circles of white paper, scissors, black felt-tip pens, glue and a silver glitter glue pen.

What to Do: The patch-work paper needs to be created first. To do this attach the white A3 paper to an easel or a tilted piece of card and run a paint-brush loaded with runny blue paint across the top edge of the paper. Encourage the paint to run and dribble down the paper by brushing across the same edge and adding either more paint or water. When several runs have been achieved, turn the paper and repeat the process along a second edge. Do this along all four edges. An irregular grid should now have been created. Once the grid is dry fill in the shapes between the lines with different shades of blue, red and pink paint that you have mixed on a card palette. Outline the shapes with a black felt-tip pen. When it is dry, cut a large candle shape out of this paper. Put blobs of blue, white and red paint on a white paper circle and use fingers to merge and spread them into a pattern. Stick the candle and the flame on the blue background paper. Add a flame shape cut from red and white paper overlaid on top of each other. Draw in the wick with a black felt-tip pen and add some radiating lines from the flame with the silver glitter glue pen. Add sequins if required around the edge.

7. Candles in a Window

Materials Needed: Green poster paper, black sugar paper, white paper, assorted green papers, gold foil, white ready mixed paint, paint-brushes, pieces of card to use as paint palettes, glue, scissors, a gold glitter glue pen and white chalk.

What to Do: Create the drip grid paper first by attaching some green poster paper to an easel or tilted piece of card and running a loaded paint-brush of runny white paint along one edge. Encourage the paint to dribble and run down the paper by repeatedly brushing across the same edge and adding more paint or water. When several runs have been achieved turn the paper and do the same along the second edge. Repeat along the remaining edges in turn. An irregular white grid on a green background should now have been created. Cut a large shape of a church window out of black paper and stick it onto a rectangular piece of white paper. Trim off the excess to retain the shape of the window before mounting it in the middle of a large piece of green poster paper. Cut some candle shapes of different sizes out of the dripped grid paper and plain green papers. Arrange them as a group at the bottom of the window frame. Add circles of different sizes cut from the same papers and gold foil. Overlay these at the top of each candle. Draw in the wicks with a felt-tip pen and add radiating lines around each one with the gold glitter glue pen. Cut the remaining drip grid paper into strips and rectangles and glue them to look like stones or bricks around the edges of the black window frame. Outline each one with a white chalk.

7. Candles in a Window

6. Patch Work Candle

THE NATIVITY

1. Bethlehem Town

Materials Needed: Large pieces of white paper, red, yellow, blue, gold, black and white ready mixed paint, sponge rollers, pieces of card to use as palettes for paint, thin strips of card, small white doilies, travel brochures or old Christmas cards showing buildings in the Holy Land as a stimulus.

What to Do: Put blobs of white, red and blue paint on a card palette, use a sponge roller to irregularly mix and pick up the colours before rolling it across the large sheet of white paper to cover it with colour. Return to the card palette to reload with paint from time to time. Allow the paint to dry before rolling a second irregular colour mix over the top. Use white red and yellow paint this time and allow patches of the first colour-cover to show through for a rich background on which to print. Use black paint and the edges of strips of card to print and drag paint to create the shapes of roofs, minarets, steps, doorways etc. after looking carefully at the buildings in travel brochures. Highlight the windows and doors by dragging white paint first and printing details on top. Drag some lines of gold ready mixed paint to echo the shapes of part of the buildings. Use a sponge roller to cover the doily with gold paint before sticking it as a star above the scene.

2. The Stable

Materials Needed: White paper, paint-brushes, pieces of card as palettes for paint, red, yellow, black and white ready mixed paint, black felt-tip pens and pictures of the stable scene as illustrated on cards and in books featuring the Nativity. The Jan Pienkowski Nativity story is an excellent source for silhouettes.

What to Do: To create the drip grid background for the stable silhouette, attach a piece of white paper to an easel or tilted piece of card, load a paint-brush with runny red paint and drag it across the top of the paper encouraging the paint to dribble and run downwards. More paint or water may need to be brushed across the same edge to achieve plenty of runs. Turn the paper and repeat the same procedure along the other three edges in turn. An irregular grid should now have been created. Once the grid is dry, fill in the shapes between the lines with different shades of red, yellow and orange that you have mixed on a card palette. Outline the filled shapes with a black felt-tip pen. Use a paint brush and black paint to draw the silhouette of a stable on this rich, brightly coloured background.

1. Bethlehem Town

2. The Stable

3. Torn Paper Figures - The Shepherds, Mary, Joseph and Baby Jesus

Materials Needed: To echo the background and simple rural lifestyle of this group of characters, earthy neutral colours of paper need to be chosen i.e. browns, greens and greys. If shapes are torn rather than cut to create these figures they will be more in keeping and sympathetic to their origins and a contrast to the affluence and richness of the kings. Pictures of these characters in books and on old Christmas cards will be needed as a stimulus. Glue and sheets of white paper as a background will also be needed.

What to Do: First tear an oval shape out of white paper as the face, then a long thick shape to be the body and two thinner and shorter shapes to be the arms. Assemble these pieces to form a figure. Before sticking them down check that they are in proportion to one another. If any are too big or too small you may need to change them before sticking the figure on to the background paper. Tear two white shapes for hands and add a head-dress of strips and shapes on the top and sides of the faces. Details on the clothing e.g. stripes can be torn and added on, as can crooks for the shepherds etc.

4. Plastic Spoon Angels

Materials Needed: White plastic spoons, white doilies, coloured paper as a background, fine black permanent markers, glue, double sided sellotape, gold pipe cleaners, gold foil and small pink pompoms.

What to Do: Fold two edges of a white doily inwards to make a large triangular shape for the body. Fold two other doilies into smaller triangles as the sleeves. Draw a face on the bowl of the plastic spoon with the permanent marker and add two pink pompoms as cheeks. Put a piece of double sided tape on the top of the spoon at the front and attach a curled and twisted gold pipe cleaner as hair. Stick a whole white doily on the background paper and assemble the previously folded doilies on it, from the middle downwards, to make the body of the angel. Slip the handle of the decorated spoon into the top of the folded body and add some gold foil circles around the head.

5. Marbled Doilies

Materials Needed: White doilies, assorted glitter glue pens, marbling inks, a shallow tray with water in it and a fork or a comb.

What to Do: Drip a few drops of about three colours of marbling ink on to the surface of the water in the tray - in this case red, yellow, and orange inks have been used. Swirl the inks around using a comb or a fork to break up any blobs and to create a pattern. Lay the doilies, one at a time, briefly on the surface of the tray before removing and placing them on newspaper to dry. If the colours on the doilies become faint, add more drops of the same coloured inks to the tray when they are dry. Decorate the doilies with lines and dots from the glitter glue pens. These marbled doilies could be displayed to effect surrounding a group of angels, over a stable scene, or as part of a massed group of stars.

6. Ribbon Wrapped Kings

Materials Needed: Wide strips of card as the kings' bodies, double sided tape, ribbon and yarn, narrow strips of white paper, pieces of cream paper, scissors, glue, black felt-tip pens, sheets of tissue paper, and white paper as a background.

What to Do: Stick a piece of double sided sellotape lengthways from the top to the bottom of both sides of a piece of card cut to the size and shape of the King's body. N.B. Only peel the backing off once this strip is stuck down and not before starting or the tape will twist and stick to itself in a tangle. Use strips of ribbon and yarn in turn to create a pattern by wrapping them around the card, the double sided tape will help to hold

3. Torn Paper Figures -
The Shepherds, Mary, Joseph
and Baby Jesus

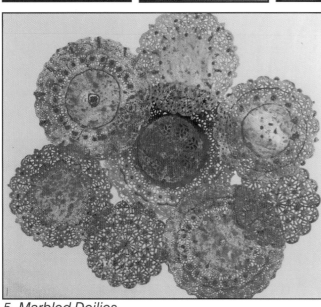

5. Marbled Doilies

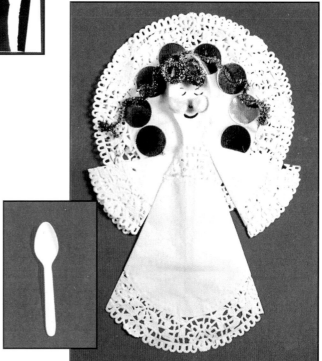

4. Plastic Spoon Angels

6. Ribbon Wrapped Kings

the pattern in place. Start and finish the ends of the yarn and ribbon by pressing them on the tape. Lay and glue a piece of tissue paper on to the white background paper. Then lay and glue the wrapped strip down the middle of the tissue paper. Fold the top of the tissue paper around the wrapped card to create a cloak effect. Cut some thin strips of ribbon as the fastening for the cloak. Add a circle of cream paper as a head above the card strip, then cut strips of ribbon and glue them down to form the shape of a crown on top of the head. Draw thin black lines on strips of white paper and arrange them as hair and a beard.

7. Adding to an Existing Design

Materials Needed: Gold foil, gold glitter glue pens, scissors, glue, pieces of white paper the same size as the picture to be used and a simple black and white picture taken from a Christmas card or book and scaled up on a photcopier to make it easier to work with.

What to Do: Talk about the existing picture, how might it be changed, what might be added to it (including where and how) and what might be taken away from it. Talk about how to create variety and interest if only one colour is used for decoration. The only stipulation needed would be that the picture must remain the same size e.g. if parts such as the black sky were to be replaced with foil the cut up rearranged picture would need to reassembled on a piece of white paper the same size as the original. A display of the different approaches and outcomes using the same picture would hopefully be a varied and interesting one. Alternatively the class could be divided into groups and each group given a different image to work on.

8. Strip Crown Designs

Materials Needed: Squares of black sugar paper as a background, scissors, glue, brown corrugated paper, gold foil, copper foil, star shapes and a single hole punch.

What to Do: Cut a strip of corrugated paper into an interesting shape as the headband of a crown and stick it across the bottom of a square of black paper. Cut other shapes from foil and corrugated paper to add to and make the head band more elaborate and crown like. Explore adding patterns to some of the shapes, using the hole punch, before gluing them down. Gift boxes could be decorated with the same materials and added to the display - as could writing, e.g. describing the presents to give to someone special.

9. The Part I Would Choose to Play

Materials Needed: Many children never get the opportunity to dress up and have a part in the school Nativity play - this is for them! Black paper, an overhead projector, red paper, gold foil, pipe cleaners, tissue paper, pompoms, vivelle etc, glue, scissors and grey paper as a background.

What to Do: First the children need to choose the character they would most like to be in the Nativity play. Then they need to find books or old Christmas cards showing that character and the type of clothes they wear. Use the overhead projector to produce the silhouette of each child's head on black paper - outline them in white chalk- ask the children to cut them out and stick them close to the bottom of a piece of grey paper. N.B. Room needs to be left for headgear and clothing around the neck. The children now decorate their own silhouette and dress themselves in the clothing they would like to wear as their chosen character. Descriptive writing could be part of this display as the children describe who they have chosen to be and the costume they would wear as this character. You might end up with 10 kings, 12 Marys etc!

7. Adding to an Existing Design

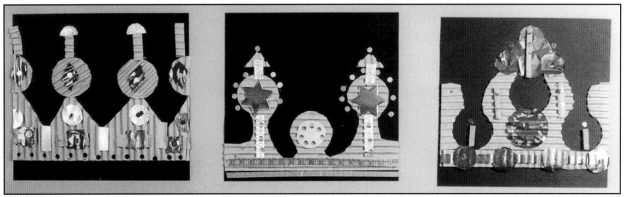

8. Strip Crown Designs

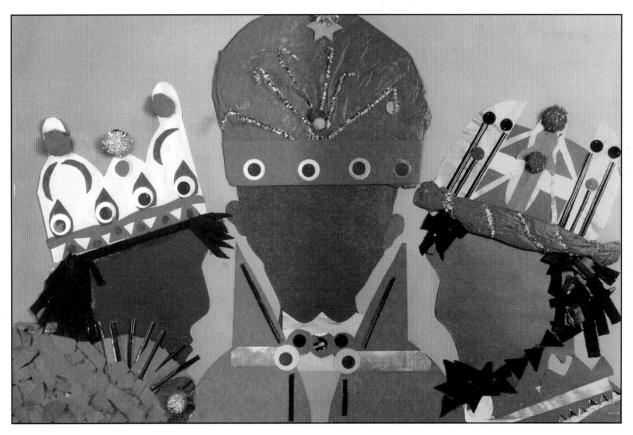

9. The Part I Would Choose to Play

STAINED GLASS WINDOWS

1. Doily Windows

Materials Needed: White doilies, black, yellow and red ready mixed paint, sponge rollers, pieces of card to use as paint palettes, glue, scissors, small red and yellow pre-cut circles, cotton-wool buds for printing, newspaper and white paper as a background.

What to Do: Lay a white doily on a piece of newspaper and with a sponge roller and black ready mixed paint, roll paint over the surface of the doily until it is completely black all over. Lift the wet doily carefully and place it to dry on a clean piece of newspaper. When the doily is dry, glue it on to a piece of white background paper. Add decoration to the doily using the red and yellow circles in a variety of ways, e.g. in groups, cut as half circles or curves etc. Look for shapes that are similar on the doily so that the arrangement of cut and stuck shapes can form a repeating pattern. Pay particular attention to the design for the centre of the doily and work outwards from it. Use a cotton wool bud and red and yellow paint to print dots and add to the cut and stuck pattern. Look for matching shapes on which to print in the same colour and maintain the idea of a repeating pattern. Print black dots around the edge of the completed window design.

2. Collage Windows from Painted Patterns

Materials Needed: Large sheets of black and white paper, paint-brushes, red, yellow and blue ready mixed paint, pieces of card to use as painting palettes, glue and scissors plus pictures of different shaped stained glass windows, e.g. on old Christmas cards, as a stimulus.

What to Do: The paper to be used for the collage needs painting first. To do this take a large sheet of white paper, a paint-brush, and two of the colours of ready mixed paint e.g. red and yellow or red and blue, and paint a series of diagonal or horizontal stripes in both colours to cover the paper. The stripes can be both broad and narrow and they need to touch each other so that none of the white paper can be seen. Leave this paper to dry. Take a large sheet of black paper and draw on it the large outline shape of a church window. Cut this shape out and stick it onto a piece of white background paper. Cut the painted paper into shapes - triangles, curves, circles, rectangles, segmented circles etc. and arrange these shapes to form patterns like stained glass window panes on the large black window shape. Leave gaps between these different shapes to look like the lead in the window. Add extra thin strips of black to create a similar effect on top of some of the large cut out shapes.

1. *Doily Windows*

2. *Collage Windows from Painted Patterns*

3. Silver, Grey, Black and White Windows

Materials Needed: Large pieces of black paper, scissors, glue, silver foil, white and grey paper, sequin waste, pencils, a silver glitter glue pen plus pictures of church window shapes as a stimulus. e.g. old Christmas cards.

What to Do: Draw a large outline shape of a church window on black paper - to make the window symmetrical it might be advisable to fold the paper first, draw half a window shape outwards from the fold, cut it out, open it up and reveal a whole window with both sides identical in shape. Fold this outline shape in half and into it cut and remove several large shapes similar to the panes observed in actual church windows. Open the shape to reveal the design - if the cut out shapes are too small or more of them are needed, refold the original shape and make some more cuts. Open up the shape (now full of cut outs) and turn it over. The papers to fill the cut outs need to be attached to the back and any surplus trimmed off before the front is decorated. Select, cut and stick pieces of the various grey, white and silver papers to fill the cut out shapes - try and build a repeating pattern in the way the collage materials are used for maximum impact. Turn the window shape over once the collage is complete, stick it on to a piece of white background paper and outline some of the shapes with the silver glitter glue pen.

4. Maths Paper Patterned Windows

Materials Needed: Coloured felt-tip pens, pencils, polar graph paper, isometrical and squared maths paper, large pieces of black paper, glue, scissors, silver glitter glue pens, pictures of church windows and stained glass designs e.g. on old Christmas cards.

What to Do: Choose one type of maths paper on which to create a pattern. Mark on it faintly with a pencil where and how the pattern will go on the paper e.g. in zig-zags, stripes etc. Choose only two or three colours of felt-tip pen to work with and colour in the pattern. Take a piece of black paper and cut out the shape of a church window and the panes in it as described in the previous example. Place this cut out frame over the coloured pattern and decide whether it needs further cutting or changing before sticking the two together and then mounting them on to the white background paper. Outline the shapes of the panes with the silver glitter glue pen.

5. Carol Singing Choir Boys

Materials Needed: White paper, black sugar paper, pink paper, glue, scissors cardboard tubes, pictures of choir boys on old Christmas cards and brightly coloured background paper.

What to do: Cut a large oval shape as the face out of white paper and stick it on to a piece of background paper. Cut into the cardboard tube to create a series of thin rings to use as eyes, noses and mouths. Explore ways of bending and squashing these for different effects and expressions before sticking them down. Infill the eye and mouth shapes with black circles. Add round pink cheeks and use strips of black paper, curled, zig zagged or folded to create a hairdo. Aim for lots of different expressions and an assorted bunch of choirboys singing their hearts out!

3. Silver, Grey, Black and White Windows

4. Maths Paper Patterned Windows

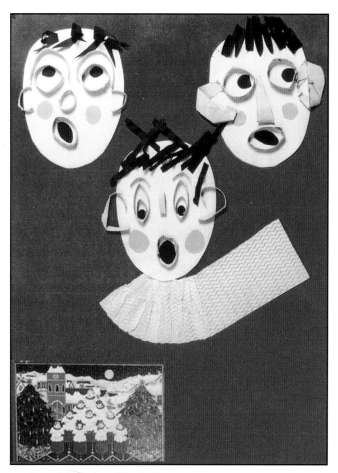

5. Carol Singing Choir Boys

1. Mixed Media Collage Panels - Christmas Cards as a Starting Point

Materials Needed: Ready mixed paint, paint-brushes, sponge rollers, scissors, glue, star templates, foil assorted papers including wall paper, fabric both patterned and plain, felt, old Christmas cards, thin ribbon and computer written greeting messages printed out. Large panels (about A3) of thin card as a background to work on.

What to Do: Choose an old Christmas card as a starting point and using the colours on it, collect papers, fabric and paint that match those colours. These materials used in different ways, e.g. by cutting, tearing, printing painting, overlaying etc. will fill your background panel in a varied and interesting way. Position the card on the background panel first and then begin filling the space around it using lots of the different materials and techniques, making sure the colours match the original card. Colour will unite the whole panel and give it impact. Display these different panels in a regular grid like arrangement as a block. Computer written greeting messages could be cut into strips and used as a border around the display.

2. Exploded Cracker Shapes

Materials Needed: White paper, sponge rollers, red, blue and white ready mixed paint, purple and cerise foil, pencils, pieces of card to use as mixing palettes, scissors, glue, a cracker template and white paper as a background.

What to Do: Take a piece of white paper, a card palette and a sponge roller. Put some blobs of red, white, and blue paint on the card and irregularly mix it with the sponge roller. Cover the white paper with colour by rolling the paint over it and leave it to dry. Then turn it over and lay the cracker template on it, draw round it and cut it out. Cut across the cracker shape in different ways to create a series of strips. These cuts need to work inwards from the edge of the cracker. Cut across one edge in a particular way and then go to the opposite edge and make a matching cut. Make a second cut - this should be different from the first- again at one edge and then at the other. Continue until the cracker is in several strips. Reassemble it into its original shape but with gaps between the strips as though it had exploded. Stick it on to a piece of white background paper. Cut another cracker out of the painted paper, keep this one whole and stick it on a piece of white background paper. Decorate it with strips and shapes cut from the foil. Arrange these crackers in rows with strips of foil at the edge of each panel.

1. Mixed Media Collage Panels - Christmas Cards as a Starting Point

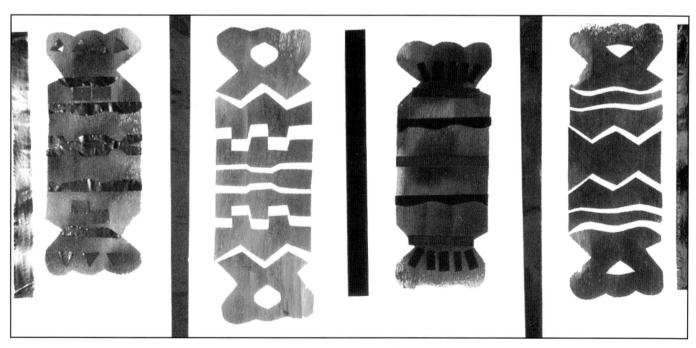

2. Exploded Cracker Shapes

atterned Parcels

Materials Needed:
Rectangles and squares of thin card as the parcel shapes, strips of green, red and white paper and silver foil, glue, scissors, white background paper, and red ribbon.

What to Do:
Choose a parcel shaped piece of card and some strips of the various coloured papers. These strips need to be arranged to form a pattern that covers the whole of the parcel. Arrange them in different ways until you have the pattern you like and want to stick down. The original strips can be cut and made smaller and arranged horizontally, vertically, diagonally, interlocking etc. to make a pattern. Add a strip of ribbon and a small bow to the finished parcel. Decorate further parcels but aim to add a different pattern to each one. If all the parcels are displayed together it should show the wealth of patterns possible if only strips are used to create them - and plenty of imagination!

4. Strip Patterned Baubles

Materials Needed:
Circles of white card as the bauble shapes, strips of red, black and white paper and silver foil, scissors, glue, white background paper and red foil.

What to Do:
Choose a circle of card and some strips of the various coloured papers. As in the previous example these strips need to be arranged to form a pattern that covers the whole of the circle. Arrange them in different ways until you have a pattern you like and want to stick down. The original strips can be cut and arranged as suggested previously. Decorate further circles but aim to add a different pattern to each one. If all the baubles are arranged together (each one suspended from a strip of black paper or red foil) it should again show a wealth of different patterns that are possible when only strips are used to make them - plus imagination!

5. Swirled Baubles

Materials Needed:
White paper as a background, red and green ready mixed paint, sponge rollers, strips of red, white, black and green paper, red foil, glue, scissors, pieces of card as palettes for paint, cotton-wool buds for printing and actual baubles with patterns on them as a stimulus.

What to Do:
Put some red paint on a card palette, load a sponge roller with the paint, place the roller on to the white background paper, press it down gently and swirl it round in a circular motion to create a bauble shape. Repeat this on other parts of of the paper to create further red baubles before doing the same with the green paint. Add decoration to each bauble by sticking different coloured strips across the middle of each one. Some of these strips could have patterns cut into them and be overlaid on top of other colours, others might have their edges altered, or have patterns of dots printed on them. Try and make the decoration on each bauble different. Cut a wavy strip of black paper for each bauble to make them all look as if they have been hung up. Small circles of red foil could be arranged among them as though they are extra baubles.

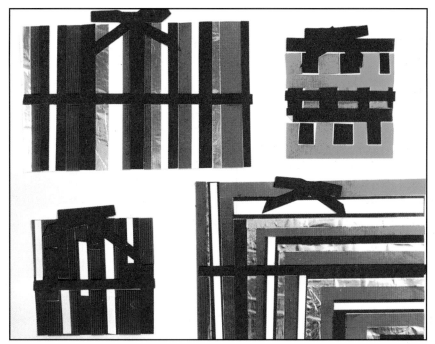

3. Patterned Parcels

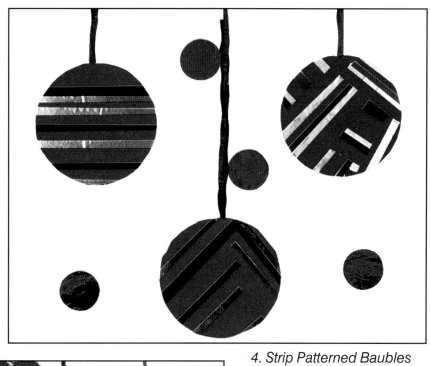

4. Strip Patterned Baubles

5. Swirled Baubles

6. Cut and Fold Baubles

Materials Needed: Purple paper, cerise foil, white background paper, purple, pink and black felt-tip pens, scissors and glue.

What to Do: Draw the outline shape of a bauble in both purple paper and foil. Fold both shapes in half and cut a series of half bauble shapes by following the outer edge of the folded bauble. These shapes will get smaller with each cut. Open all the shapes out, rearrange and combine some of them i.e. shapes inside shapes to form a new bauble on a piece of white background paper. Combine foil shapes and the ones from the purple paper to make the bauble. Leave gaps between the shapes inside the bauble - you wont need to use all the ones you have cut. Patterns can be drawn in these gaps using the felt-tip pens. Make other bauble shapes and decorate them in different ways and with different patterns.

7. Printed Baubles

Materials Needed: White paper circles, circular lids, cotton wool buds, thin strips of card, draught excluder, red and green ready mixed paint, paint-brushes and pieces of card to use as paint palettes.

What to Do: Print a pattern to decorate a white paper circle after first considering how the pattern might be arranged e.g. in strips, as a circular design etc. Look carefully at the range of materials and consider ways they could be combined e.g. shapes inside shapes, shapes between shapes etc to make the pattern more interesting. Simple printing blocks can be made from the draught excluder. Cut it into strips and arrange it to make a shape on the outer flat top of an aerosol lid. Remove the plastic covering if there is any, dab on paint with a brush and print. Strips of green and red paper could be included in the pattern as well if desired. The use of only red and green paint for the patterns will give the final display greater impact.

8. Rolled and Printed Baubles

Materials Needed: Circles of white paper, red, yellow and gold ready mixed paint, sponge rollers, pieces of card as mixing palettes, cotton wool buds and cotton bobbins for printing with.

What to Do: Mix together on a piece of card some blobs of red and yellow paint using a sponge roller. Aim for an irregular, uneven mix before covering a circle of white paper with colour using the roller. When the paint is dry, add a pattern to the circle by drawing curves and lines with fingers and gold ready mixed paint and adding printed shapes and dots with bobbins and cotton wool buds.

9. Collage and Printed Baubles

Materials Needed: Black paper, pencils, silver foil, white ready mixed paint, cotton wool buds for printing, pieces of card to use as paint palettes, glue, scissors, a silver glitter glue pen and actual baubles as a stimulus for shapes and decorative patterns.

What to do: Fold a piece of black paper in half, and from the fold draw half a bauble shape and cut it out. Open the shape to reveal the whole symmetrical bauble shape. Add decoration to this bauble using cut foil shapes, printed white dots and lines and shapes drawn with a glitter glue pen. Work across the middle of the bauble first before adding pattern to the top and bottom of it. Additional baubles can be worked in the same way - aim to make the pattern different on each one for interest and variation. Mount the finished baubles on a red background to add colour and richness to the display

6. Cut and Fold Baubles

7. Printed Baubles

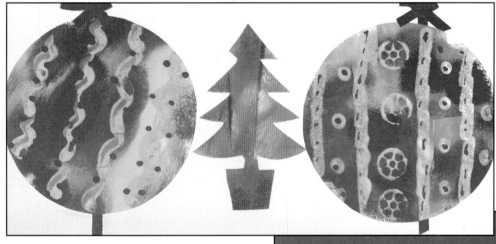

8. Rolled and
Printed Baubles

9. Collage and Printed
Baubles

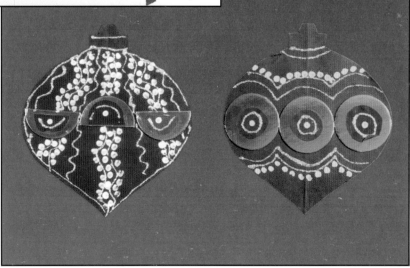

TREES

1. Using Different Shades of Green

Materials Needed: Christmas tree templates, oil pastel crayons, blue, white and yellow ready mixed paint, pieces of card as mixing palettes, paint-brushes and large sheets of white paper.

What to Do: Draw round the Christmas tree template with a green oil pastel crayon in several different places on the white paper. Arrange the tree at a different angle each time and leave plenty of space between the trees. Older children could draw and cut out their own templates rather than be provided with one. Mix lots of different shades of green paint on the card palette, and use each shade in turn to follow the outline of one or more trees. Aim eventually to cover all the white paper except for the tree shapes themselves. When the paint is dry use white and green oil pastel crayons to add extra outlines around the trees. A group of these arranged tightly next to each other and unmounted would make a stunning wall display.

2. Strip Patterned Trees

Materials Needed: White triangular card shapes of different sizes, scissors, glue, strips of green paper in a variety of shades and white paper as a background.

What to Do: Choose a triangle of card and some strips of the various coloured papers. These strips need to be arranged to form a pattern that covers the whole of the triangle. Arrange them in different ways until you have the pattern you like and want to stick down. The original strips can be cut and made smaller and arranged, horizontally, vertically, diagonally, interlocking etc. to make a pattern. Decorate further triangular tree shapes but aim to add a different pattern to each one. Display the trees as a group on white background paper. They will hopefully show the wealth of patterns that are possible if only strips are used to create them - plus imagination!

3. Torn Paper Trees

Materials Needed: Large sheets of green paper as a background, strips of white paper, pencils, a single hole punch and snowflake punch, glue, different shades of green paper for tearing - old wall paper is ideal as it leaves a white edge when it is torn- small pieces (A4 size) of green paper, brown paint and a paint-brush.

What to Do: Draw the faint outline shape of a Christmas tree and its trunk on a piece of green A4 paper, portrait way up. Tear some strips of wallpaper and glue them to follow and fill the shape of the tree, overlap the torn strips to add both colour and texture. Paint the trunk brown. Cut out the finished tree carefully and stick it on the green background paper. Surround it with other torn and cut strips in different shades of green. Punch patterns in some of the strips using the different hole punches. Use the punched out circles as snowflakes falling next to the trees.

1. Using Different Shades of Green

2. Strip Patterned Trees

3. Torn Paper Trees

...ecorated Tree

...ed: Large sheets of black paper, pencils, scissors, glue, long strips of red, yellow and orange paper and gold foil, plus gold paper as a background.

...t to do: Fold a large piece of black paper in half, and from the fold draw half a triangular shaped Christmas tree plus its trunk. Cut it out carefully and open the shape to reveal a whole symmetrical Christmas tree. Choose several strips of the different coloured papers and experiment with changing one or both edges of each (top and bottom) in different ways i.e. by cutting out rows of different shapes. Lay the strips across the black tree shape with gaps between them. Stick them down and trim off any bits that overhang the edge of the tree by turning the tree over and cutting carefully along the tree edge. Mount the tree on gold background paper and for display choose another paper e.g. red that matches one of the colours used for the strips.

5. Trees With Cut Out Patterns

Materials Needed: Brightly coloured paper as a background (in this case orange), glue, scissors, black paper, a Christmas tree template (provided or drawn by the children themselves), pencils and a gold glitter glue pen.

What to Do: Place the tree template on a piece of black paper, draw round it and cut it out carefully. Fold it in half, or in thirds and cut out similar shapes along each vertical fold. Leave plenty of fold uncut so that the tree shape remains intact. Open the tree shape up to reveal the pattern. Draw round and cut out several further trees. Fold and cut patterns into each one. Try to make each tree different by varying the folds or the shapes cut out. Stick the trees on to the brightly coloured background paper and add further decoration to them using the gold glitter glue pen.

6. Trees Inside Hollow Shapes

Materials Needed: Orange, green and white paper, dark green background paper, pencils, scissors, glue, red, white and green ready mixed paint, cotton wool buds for printing, pieces of card to use as paint palettes, Christmas tree templates, large margarine tubs or lids to draw round.

What to Do: Choose a piece of coloured paper, place a rectangular margarine tub on it, draw round the shape and cut it out. Fold the cut out shape in half and following the edge carefully cut out a smaller shape from inside it. Open the now hollow shape up and stick it on a piece of green background paper. Draw round the Christmas tree template on a different coloured paper and cut it out carefully. Stick the tree shape on the background paper inside the hollow shape. Add strings of lights to the tree by printing dots with paint and a cotton wool bud. Display the finished trees in rows.

7. Trees with "U" shaped Cuts

Materials Needed: Green paper, white paper, green foil, green tissue paper, pencils, scissors and glue.

What to Do: Fold a piece of green paper in half, draw a triangular Christmas tree on it outwards from the fold - include the trunk as well. Cut the shape out carefully, keep the shape folded and cut "u" shaped cuts at intervals down the outside of the tree shape. Leave plenty of the centre fold intact and remove the "u" shapes each time. The cuts will get longer as you work down the tree. Open the cut tree - it will now have rib shapes down it rather like a skeleton. Mount this on green tissue paper and add a few cut out circles of white or green foil as snow or decorations. An alternative to this colour

4. Cut Strip Decorated Tree

5. Trees With Cut Out Patterns

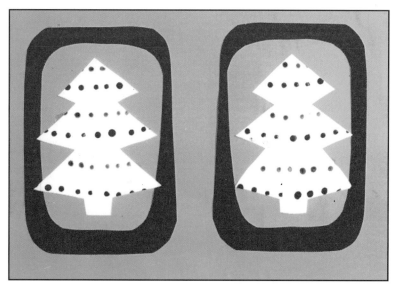

6. Trees Inside Hollow Shapes

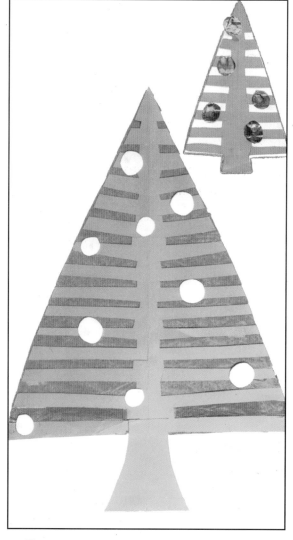

7. Trees with "U" shaped Cuts

scheme would be to cut the trees out of black or white paper and mount each one on a different colour of tissue paper - as though they were trees with fairy lights on them. Grouped together they would make a stunning display.

8. Rolled Paint Trees

Materials Needed: Large pieces of white paper, triangles of white card to use as stencils, strips of card for printing, sponge rollers, yellow, blue, black and white ready mixed paint, and pieces of card to use as mixing palettes.

What to Do: Make an irregular mix of different shades of green on the card palette with paint and a sponge roller. Place a card triangle on the white background paper and roll the sponge roller loaded with green paint across it, move the triangle and repeat on another part of the background. Continue working this way, building up a group of overlapping white triangles both large and small on a rolled green background. Outline the shapes with black lines printed with the edge of a strip of card. Drag thicker lines as the trunks for the trees. Print white snowflakes with fingers among the trees.

9. Marbled and Wax Resist Trees

Materials Needed: White paper, marbling inks, a shallow tray, a fork or a comb, wax crayons, coloured drawing inks, paint-brushes, scissors, glue and glitter glue pens.

What to Do: Half fill the shallow tray with water and drip a few drops of two or three colours of marbling ink onto the surface of the water. Swirl the inks around with an old fork or comb to mix and mingle the colours and break up any blobs. Check that the paper is the right size for the tray before laying it briefly on the surface of the inky water. Lift the paper off to reveal the print and allow it to dry. Take a second print from the same tray (it will be fainter than the first) before adding more ink and taking another print. When the marbling is dry, cut it into a series of triangular shapes as trees. When producing the wax resist paper for the other trees, work in colours that are similar to the marbling inks e.g. if orange, red and yellow marbling has been produced, use orange red or yellow crayon for the wax scribble and wash over it with either red, yellow or orange ink. It should then really glow and complement the marbled trees when they are grouped together. Cut this paper into triangular shapes as well and arrange them in an overlapping group with the marbled trees. Add plain paper trees or cellophane trees if extra colour is desired. Draw in or add sticky paper trunks to the trees and use the glitter glue pens to add swirls or lines in the sky.

10. Corrugated Paper Trees

Materials Needed: Red and green plain paper, red green and brown corrugated paper, pencils, a Christmas tree template, strips of red and green paper and gold foil, a single hole punch, tartan wrapping paper, gold snowflakes, squares of white card as background paper, glue and scissors.

What to Do: Take a square of background paper and cover it with plain paper or a tartan wrapping paper. Cut strips of brown corrugated paper and stick them as a border around the edge of the square. Stick either strips of red or strips of green paper on top of the right and left hand border corrugated strips. Punch holes in two gold strips with the single hole punch and stick them on top of the coloured strips. Draw round and cut a Christmas tree shape out of corrugated paper - any colour - and arrange in the centre of the square. Decorate the tree with a few purchased ready made snowflake shapes. Using the same materials and the same basic design several different colour combinations can be explored.

8. Rolled Paint Trees

9. Marbled and Wax Resist Trees

10. Corrugated Paper Trees

43

11. Patterns Behind Trees

Materials Needed: Squares of white paper, strips of coloured paper in two colours only (here red and green have been combined for one design and green and blue for the other) pieces of green paper, scissors, glue, white ready mixed paint and oil pastel crayons.

What to do: Take a square of white background paper and on it arrange a pattern of strips either horizontally or vertically across it with gaps between the strips. Use dots of white finger prints and further lines drawn in oil pastel to add extra patterns on and between the strips. Draw round and cut out a Christmas tree shape to stick in the middle of the pattern.

12. Yarn Wrapped Christmas Tree

Materials Needed: Triangles of card as the trees, double sided sellotape, red yarn, silver sequins or a glitter glue pen, squares of white card as a background, grey poster paper with a drip grid pattern on it - how to make this type of pattern is described in an earlier example (turn to stars number 7 on page 10) - squares of black paper, thin strips of red paper, scissors and glue.

What to Do: Put a strip of double sided tape vertically down the back of a card triangle and do not remove the backing from it until the strip is stuck down or it will tangle. Press the end of a piece of yarn on to the tape and then wrap it in a random design around the card triangle. The double sided tape will help hold the wrapping in place. Cut a square of dripped grid paper and mount it on a black square and stick it in the middle of the white card background. Stick the yarn wrapped Christmas tree in the middle of the grey square. Decorate the yarn with blobs of glitter glue or stick on a few sequins. Cut some strips of grey paper and with the red paper strips make a pattern of diagonal stripes across each corner of the square. Add a couple of blobs of glitter glue or sequins as well.

13. Drip Grid Christmas Tree

Materials Needed: White paper, paint brushes, blue, white and yellow ready mixed paint, pieces of card to use as mixing palettes, black felt-tip pens, thin strips of white paper, yellow paper, a gold glitter glue pen, gold stars, scissors, glue, cotton wool buds for printing and sheets of green and black paper.

What to Do: To create the coloured drip grid paper for the tree attach a piece of white paper to an easel or tilted piece of card, mix some green paint and follow the directions given previously in: The Stable, number 2 on page 22. Fill in the grid with different shades of green and outline it with a black felt-tip pen. Cut a large Christmas tree shape out of the green grid and mount it on a piece of black paper. Cut the tree shape out again leaving a narrow black margin around it and mount it on a piece of green paper. Add strips of white paper as candles and pieces of white paper as parcels. Give each candle a black wick drawn on a yellow circle. Add some gold stars and some rows of green and white dots as lights printed with paint and a cotton wool bud. Add some glitter glue lines radiating around each candle flame.

11. Patterns Behind Trees

12. Yarn Wrapped Christmas Tree

13. Drip Grid Christmas Tree

IN THE STYLE OF OTHER ARTISTS

1. The Virgin Mary in the Style of Modigliani

Materials Needed: Postcards and large pictures of portraits by Modigliani in order to become familiar with his style (elongated, thin faces and features). Old Christmas cards and books that show the Virgin Mary and the type of clothing she might have worn. Sheets of white paper and chalk pastel crayons.

What to Do: Practise drawing with a finger on a piece of white paper the outline of the head of your portrait - to get a feel of the size it will be and how it will fit on and fill the paper allowing room for its shoulders and headdress. Draw a faint outline of your portrait with a pale coloured chalk pastel. Look carefully at the way Modigliani drew facial features and add features to your portrait in the same style. Sketch in the clothing before adding and filling your drawing and the background with colour. Fix the finished chalk pastel drawing with hairspray to prevent it from smudging.

2. The Shepherds in the Style of Monet

Materials Needed: Postcards and large pictures of paintings by Monet in order to become familiar with his style (merging colours and a limited use of definite outlines). Pictures of shepherds their clothing and their setting as shown on old Christmas cards and books. Pieces of white paper and chalk pastel crayons.

What to Do: Sketch out your group of shepherds with a finger to get a feel for their size and arrangement on the piece of white paper. Then draw the group faintly with a pale coloured chalk pastel. Work in the sky around and above the figures by smudging and blending some of the colour - use fingers or a paper towel for this. Next add colour and limited detail 'Monet style' to the figures themselves before filling in the setting around and beneath them. Blend and smudge some of the colour as before. Fix the finished pastel drawing with hairspray to prevent it from smudging.

3. A King in the Style of Picasso

Materials Needed: Postcards and larger pictures of portraits by Picasso particularly those showing strong, bold features. Pictures of kings in books and on old Christmas cards. Pieces of white paper and chalk pastel crayons.

What to Do: Draw the outline of the head of your king with a finger on the piece of white paper to get a feel for the size it will need to be to fill the paper leaving enough room for its shoulders and headwear. Sketch your portrait with a pale coloured pastel. Add colour and detail to the headwear first before adding features to the face. These need to be bold and stand out with defined black outlines. Add and fill the collar of the kings costume with strong colour and more black outlines. Fix the finished pastel drawing with hair spray to prevent it from smudging.

1. *Gypsy Woman with Baby in the Style of Modigliani*

2. *The Shepherds in the Style of Monet*

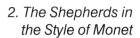

3. *A King in the Style of Picasso*

4. I Saw Three Ships in the Style of Van Gogh

Materials Needed: Postcards and larger pictures of work by Van Gogh that show his style (strong colour and vigorous lines). Illustrations of the carol as shown in music books and on old Christmas cards. Pieces of white paper and chalk pastel crayons.

What to Do: Sketch your group of three ships on the piece of white paper with a finger to get a feel for the size they will need to be and how they will fit on the paper. Next sketch an outline of them with a pale coloured chalk pastel. Work on filling the sky first - remembering to use strong colour and bold marks. Add colour and detail to the boats next before adding a sea full of strong moving lines, shapes and colours. Fix the finished pastel drawing with hair spray to prevent it from smudging.

5. Eastern Background Scene in the Style of Paul Klee

Materials Needed: Postcards and larger pictures of the work of Paul Klee after his visit to North Africa. These are to give a feeling for his style and how he combined the shapes and colours of that part of the world. Pieces of white paper, pieces of scrap paper and chalk pastels.

What to do: Collect the colours from the pastel box that most closely match the colours used by Paul Klee. Explore blending pastels together on a piece of scrap paper to make those colours that you cannot match. On a white piece of paper with a pale coloured chalk pastel sketch your own combination of shapes that are similar to the ones used by Paul Klee. Fill these shapes with Paul Klee colours. Over draw with a black pastel some of the outlines of buildings in a similar way to Paul Klee. Fix the finished pastel drawing with hair spray to prevent it from smudging.

6. Poinsettias in the Style of Louis Comfort Tiffany

Materials Needed: Actual poinsettia plants for initial observational work, postcards and pictures of glass designs by Tiffany to become familiar with his style (strong colours, bold shapes and black outlines). Pencils, pieces of grey sugar paper, black felt-tip pens, and a choice of oil pastel or chalk pastel crayons. Viewfinders and scrap pieces of paper.

What to Do: Look through a viewfinder at the different parts of the poinsettia plant to gather information about the shapes involved and how they join together. Make several quick sketches on scrap paper of the different parts. Choose either oil pastels or chalk pastels to work with and select the colours that match the poinsettia plant. On a piece of grey sugar paper faintly sketch out with a pale coloured chalk pastel a large drawing of a poinsettia. Fill the shapes with the appropriate colours using either oil or chalk pastel crayon. Outline the shapes with strong black lines in pastel or felt-tip pen before beginning work on the background. Divide this into shapes 'Tiffany' style and fill the shapes with different shades of blue before adding black outlines as before.

4. I Saw Three
Ships in the Style
of Van Gogh
(with kind permission
of State Pushkin
Museum of Fine Arts)

5. Eastern Background
Scene in the Style of
Paul Klee

6. Poinsettias in the Style
of Louis Comfort Tiffany

7. Holly and Ivy Patterns in the Style of William Morris

Materials Needed: Postcards and larger pictures of wallpaper and textile designs by William Morris that feature plants, to become familiar with his style (plant shapes that repeat and are joined to create patterns in a variety of ways). In many cases the plants have been altered from those originally observed to create a richer, more complex pattern. Holly and Ivy leaves for observational drawing, pencils and scrap pieces of paper. Red or green squares of paper as a background, white paper, gold foil, small pieces of green paper, scissors, glue and a gold glitter glue pen.

What to Do: Choose either a holly or ivy leaf and make several quick sketches of it to become familiar with its shape. Choose foil or coloured paper, draw several of your leaf shapes on it (on the back) and cut them out. Choose a square of background paper and arrange your leaf shapes on it 'William Morris' style. You may need to try several arrangements before you have the one you want to stick down. Next cut and arrange some shapes that will link your leaves together and extend the pattern. Add further decoration using the glitter glue pen - work from the top of your pattern downwards to avoid smudging.

8. Winter Tree in the Style of Mondrian

Materials Needed: Postcards and larger pictures of trees painted by Piet Mondrian to become familiar with his style (strong linear shapes on a coloured background), pencils, viewfinders, black and white ready mixed paint, paint-brushes, pieces of card to use as mixing palettes, thin strips of card for printing, pieces of grey sugar paper, scrap pieces of white paper and a silver glitter glue pen.

What to Do: Use a viewfinder to collect information about actual tree shapes and how they fit together. Make several quick observed drawings of different parts of actual trees. If there are not any trees nearby, use photographs instead. Mix several different shades of grey with a brush on a card palette. Use these greys to cover a large sheet of grey sugar paper. Aim for swirls and patches of the different greys that merge together but on the whole remain separate. An all over coverage of the same shade needs to be avoided! Allow the paint to dry and experiment with printing curved and straight lines on a scrap piece of paper, using black paint and the edge of a piece of card. Try dragging the paint with the card as well to create thicker lines. Use the different lines that you can now print to copy some of the shapes in your observational drawing and create a large strong 'Mondrian style' tree shape on the grey background. Decide where the thick lines should be before building up a mass of curved and straight overlapping branches spreading outwards. Add some thin silver lines to the finished tree with the glitter glue pen.

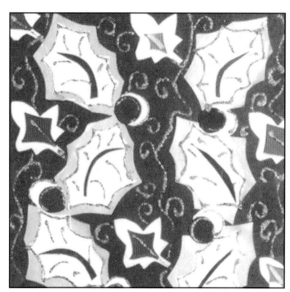

7. Holly and Ivy Patterns in the Style of William Morris

8. Winter Tree in the Style of Mondrian

PLANTS

1. Swirls and Printed Holly

Materials Needed:
Black paper as a background, blue, white and yellow ready mixed paint, sponge rollers, pieces of card to use as mixing palettes, thin strips of card for printing, red paper and foil, real holly leaves, scissors and glue.

What to Do:
Put some blobs of blue and yellow paint on a piece of card and with a sponge roller mix the colours together to create different shades of green. Place the loaded roller on the black background paper, press it down gently and swirl it round to create a green circle. Add further circles in the same way, returning when necessary to the palette for more paint. Build up a mass of overlapping swirls in the centre of the paper leaving a margin of black paper around the edge. Cut some small circles of red paper and foil and stick them down in scattered groups as holly berries. Take a thin piece of card, curve it slightly, dip it into either white or green paint and after looking at the curves on actual holly leaves, print similar curves to build up leaf shapes on the swirled background between and around the groups of berries. Finally print in a centre vein on each leaf shape.

2. Swirled, Collaged and Printed Holly Wreath

Materials Needed:
White paper as a background, blue, yellow, black and white ready mixed paint, sponge rollers, pieces of card to use as mixing palettes, thin strips of card for printing, red and green paper, scissors, glue, pencils, red ribbon and actual holly leaves.

What to Do:
Draw a large circle on the white background paper. Put blobs of blue and yellow paint on a card palette and with the sponge roller mix them together to make different shades of green. Put the loaded roller on to the pencil line you have drawn to outline the circle, press it down gently and swirl it round to create a circle of green. Add further circles in the same way, each one on the circle outline. This will make the wreath shape. These circles need to be close together and to touch one another. Cut some circles of red paper and foil and add them in scattered groups around the wreath. Take a thin strip of card, curve it slightly and after looking at the curves on the edge of a holly leaf, use black and white paint to print similar curves and build up holly leaf shapes on and protruding from the wreath. Cut some holly leaves out of green paper and add these to the wreath following its circular shape carefully. Add a bow of thin red ribbon to the bottom of the wreath.

3. Painted Holly Berries and Leaves

Materials Needed:
Pieces of white paper as a background, red, blue and yellow ready mixed paint, paint-brushes, pieces of card to use as mixing palettes, red and green oil pastel crayons and pictures of holly or actual holly.

What to Do:
Put a blob of red paint on the card palette and with a paint-brush paint a group of large overlapping holly berries on a piece of white background paper. Use some yellow and blue paint to mix one shade of green on the card palette. Use this with a brush to draw and fill several large holly leaf shapes branching out from the berries. Mix several further shades of green and use each one in turn to add an outline to the filled in leaf shapes. Continue adding outlines and then filling the gaps left until the paper is full of different shades of green. Use the oil pastel crayons to add detail and further outlines to both the berries and the leaves.

1. Swirls and Printed Holly

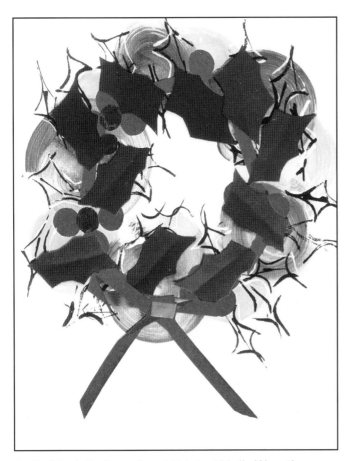

2. Swirled, Collaged and Printed Holly Wreath

3. Painted Holly Berries and Leaves

4. Ivy Leaves

Materials Needed: Pieces of white paper as a background, yellow, black and blue ready mixed paint, pieces of card as mixing palettes, sponge rollers, green tissue paper, gold foil, pencils, green and white paper, scissors, strips of card for printing, glue and actual ivy leaves.

What to Do: Put some blobs of yellow and blue paint on a card palette, mix them together with a roller to produce an uneven mix of different shades of green. Run the loaded roller vertically up and down the white background to cover it with the greens. Tear some rectangular shapes from the green paper and the tissue paper and stick them randomly on the painted background. Tear some strips of gold foil and add it to some of the shapes. Draw and cut out ivy leaves from white and green paper after looking at the shapes of real ivy leaves. Arrange these in overlapping pairs on the painted and torn background. Use the edge of a strip of card and black ready mixed paint to print outlines and veins on some of the leaves.

5. Swirls and Mistletoe

Materials Needed: White background paper, sponge rollers, yellow, white and blue ready mixed paint, strips of card for printing, paper clips, cotton-wool buds, green paper, scissors, glue, pieces of card as mixing palettes and pictures of mistletoe.

What to Do: Put blobs of yellow and blue ready mixed paint on to a card palette and with a sponge roller mix the colours to make different shades of green. Put the loaded roller on to the background paper, press it down gently and swirl it round to create a green circle. Add further circles in the same way, returning to the palette for more paint when necessary. Build up a mass of overlapping circles. Add some pairs of white mistletoe berries to the background using finger prints and white ready mixed paint. Take a strip of card, make a loop with it, fasten the ends together with a paper clip and use this loop shape, dipped in green paint to add pairs of leaves to the berries. Cut out further pairs of similar smaller leaf shapes from green paper to go on top of them. Add dots to the end of each berry with a cotton wool bud and green paint.

6. Fold, Print and Cut Poinsettias

Materials Needed: Pieces of red, green and white paper, white background paper, red and green and black ready mixed paint, paint-brushes, scissors, glue, gold foil, a gold glitter glue pen and an actual poinsettia plant.

What to Do: Look at the red and green areas on the flower heads of the poinsettia. Fold some white paper in half. Run red paint down approximately three quarters the length of the inside of the fold. Run green paint down the remaining length of the fold. Press one half of the paper down on top of the other, smoothing it together from the fold. Open it up to reveal a symmetrical red and green print. Do the same with the red paper but only use green paint at one end of the fold. When you have made several prints, look at the poinsettia petal shapes and cut individual petal shapes out of each print. Arrange the petals in groups each group radiating from a central point to resemble the real plant. Add gold foil circles to the centre of each group and some lines of gold glitter glue to the petals. Cut out some green leaves to add to the background and paint in some strong black swirls. This works very successfully as a large scale collaborative piece of work.

7. Drip grid Poinsettias and Holly

Materials Needed: White, green and red paper, pieces of white background paper, scissors, glue, paint-brushes, pieces of card as mixing palettes, red, white, yellow and blue ready mixed paint and black felt-tip pens.

What to Do: Produce the red and green drip grid material first - turn to number 7 on page 10. Use this material combined with the plain green and red paper to cut up and create holly and poinsettia plants on a white background.

4. Ivy Leaves

5. Swirls and Mistletoe

7. Drip grid Poinsettias and Holly

6. Fold, Print and
Cut Poinsettias

3D WORK

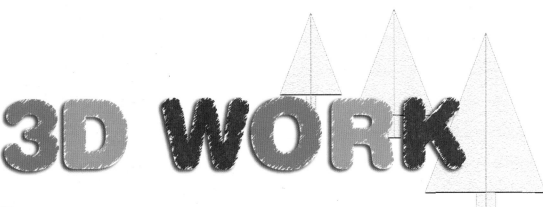

1. Slotted Trees

Materials Needed:

Cardboard tubes, thin (4sheet) card or coloured corrugated paper, glue, safety snips (to cut the slits in the tube - this part could be done by an adult) plain coloured paper, scissors, paint.

What to do:

Draw a large triangle on the sheet of card or corrugated paper to resemble the shape of a Christmas tree and cut the shape out. Cut two slits, one on either side of the top of the cardboard tube and slot the bottom of the triangular shape into it. You have now created your tree (test it to see if it will stand upright and that the trunk and the top are in proportion to one another). Remove the card triangle to decorate it - this could be done by adding printed snowflakes using paint and a cotton wool bud or gluing on cut strips of coloured paper (in a limited range of colours) or using papers coloured in a previous session i.e. by marbling or using a sponge roller to merge colours. The tube trunk could be painted or covered with a plain paper. Return the decorated triangle to its slit add further decoration if desired e.g. circles of foil or stars, and your tree is complete. For display it could form part of a collaborative free standing forest on a flat surface or become a table decoration.

2 Cone Trees

Materials Needed:

Plain coloured paper, thin card or corrugated paper (green or black), pencil, scissors, a circular shape to draw round (paper plates are ideal) glue, paper clips, foil and coloured papers to use for decoration.

What to do:

Place the circular shape on the plain green or black paper and draw round it. Cut the circle out and fold it in half. To make a cone either curl the folded shape round and fasten the bottom edges as they meet with a paper clip or cut the folded circle in half and create two trees by fastening each one together in the same way with a paper clip. Alternatively they could be glued along the join. To decorate the trees, foil and coloured paper should be used and several possibilities explored before the final effect is created and glued into place. This might include cutting and curling paper, wrapping long strips round the shape from the top of the cone or cutting a spiral into a paper circle and dropping it over the cone - the possibilities are endless. As with the slotted trees these could be displayed in a similar way.

3. Cone Figures

Materials Needed:

Plain coloured paper,pencil, circular shape to draw round, scissors, glue, thin card squares (21x21 cm approx), double sided tape, white plastic spoons, black permanent marker, doilies, foil and assorted papers to use for decoration. Old Christmas cards for ideas for figures.

What to do:

Decide on the figure you want to make and find Christmas cards showing that figure to get ideas for clothing, features etc. Consider the main colour your figure wears e.g. red for Father Christmas and construct a cone in that colour using the same

1. Slotted Trees

2. Cone Trees

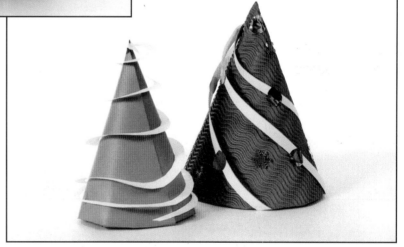

3. Cone Figures

57

method as for the trees above. Attach your cone to a card base using double sided tape i.e.put some strips of tape on the card base and press the cone down on top of them. Cut across the top of the cone to create a hole for the handle of the plastic spoon to pass through leaving the bowl of the spoon sticking up as the head. Draw features on this to create a face using the permanent marker. Add hair, and further clothing using different papers. Arms can be created by sticking a strip around the figure and adding a hand at either end. Poetry or creative writing relating to each figure could be displayed behind the finished figures.

4. Folded Figures

Materials Needed: Thin white card A4 size (4 sheet thickness) or corrugated paper, scissors, pencil, glue, foil and other coloured papers for decoration, ready mixed paint, card pieces as palettes and brushes. Old Christmas cards showing snowmen, kings, angels etc. for ideas.

What to do: Fold the A4 card in half lengthwise, keep it folded whilst you mark 2cm out from the top of the centre fold and then 14 cm up from the base of the unfolded edge. Join these two marks in a curve to create a body shape, cut along the curve. Fold a smaller piece of card (8 to 9 cm long) in half and again keeping it folded draw and cut a curve from top to bottom to create a head. Paint the folded body shape or decorate it with papers produced in a previous session e.g. by wax resist. Add further collage decoration along the base of the body before attaching the head - the fold of the head will need to be glued along the top of the fold of the body. Add crowns, hats, hair and other features using other papers and a range of cutting and folding skills. Paint a simple black silhouette on a separate piece of paper to be displayed behind each completed figure or group of figures, e.g. a stable, palm trees, a house. The figures themselves could be displayed standing upright on shelves made from box lids stapled to the wall.

5. A Cone Crown

Materials Needed: White card A3 size if possible (4 sheet thickness), black sugar paper, a large circular shape to draw round, gold foil, gold card or gold corrugated paper (corrugated border roll is ideal), scissors, glue, maths shapes to draw round to create decorative details. Sellotape or double sided tape.

What to do: Place the large circular shape on the white card, draw round it and cut it out. Fold the circle in half, cut it in half and as with the cone figures curl it round until the edges meet and a cone shape has been created. Glue or tape the seam together, a paper clip is a useful means of holding the seam together whilst the glue dries. There are many ways this cone can be decorated and made into an elaborate crown. The one illustrated has had slits cut into the top of the cone, the triangular shapes created have been folded back and decorated and other strips have been attached to the inside of the top and curved back on themselves before being stuck back on the body of the cone. A strip of border roll, slightly folded and attached around and under the base of cone makes a brim which has further decorative shapes added to it. The possibilities are endless - and hopefully individual!

6. A Strip Crown

Materials Needed: The same as the cone crown but without the circular shape to draw round.

What to Do: Cut the A3 card into strips lengthways, approx 7 to 8 cm in width. Use one strip as a head band, attach the others in turn by fastening each end to the band but allowing them to stand up above it e.g. one could go from front to back another from side to side. The strips will cross over one another to make a framework and can finally be fastened together at the top with glue or paper clips. This shape is now ready for

4. Folded Figures

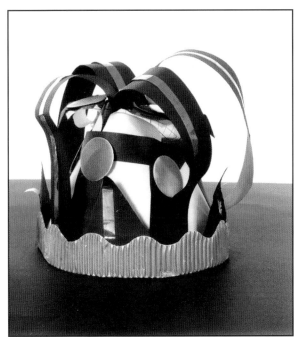

5. A Cone Crown

6. A Strip Crown

elaboration and decoration using additional cut shapes and paper skills. If the colour scheme for the class or group crown making was limited as in the illustrations i.e. black, white and gold, the children would find the limited choice helpful in making decisions about extra shapes and decoration. Too much choice can confuse! The final display too would benefit from the impact of limited colour.

7. Paper Plate Baubles

Materials Needed: Two white paper plates per bauble (large size), scissors, glue, silver foil and red poster or sticky paper cut into narrow strips and shapes, black sugar paper, red and black ready mixed paint, cotton wool buds, pieces of cut card as palettes, paper clips, small white card or paper pre-cut circles and stars to use as central motifs (older children could design and cut out their own central motifs).

What to do: Cover one of the paper plates with black sugar paper or black paint. Cut the centre circle out of the second plate leaving a fairly wide circular rim intact. Turn this circular rim over so that it is raised up and place it edge to edge on top of the black plate. Glue the edges of both plates together and use a few paper clips to hold these edges together until the glue takes purchase - remove them when it has dried and feels firm. The bauble shape has now been made and is ready for decoration. The black inner circle needs decorating first. Choose a central motif and add extra decoration to it e.g. using cut strips, printing with a cotton wool bud - or fingers! Cut and stick strips - (or shapes or both) to create a bold repeating pattern round the circular band of the top plate, add further fine detail by printing with a cotton wool bud or fingers first around the inner and then the outer rim of the top plate. To display these, cut some strips of red crepe paper and fasten them to the display board as though they were ribbons hanging down. Use a variety of different lengths for interest. Cut a V shape into the end of each ribbon. Attach a red crepe bow to the top of each strip. Glue or pin each completed bauble onto the strips at different levels. You may need to fasten more than one bauble on some strips. Unified colour and individual designs should give this display considerable impact.

8. Paper Strip Fantasy Baubles

Materials Needed: A4 and A3 thin white card (4 sheet thickness), glue, scissors, tissue paper, foil, art straws, paper clips, squares of white card to fasten the baubles to - the size of the each base will depend on the size of each individual bauble made.

What to Do: Choose a sheet of either A4 or A3 white card and cut it into strips lengthwise. The strips should be 2 to 3cm wide. Make each strip into a band i.e. a circle by gluing the ends together - use paper clips to keep them intact until the glue takes purchase. Pass the bands over one another to form a ball-like structure, join the top of the ball together with glue and paper clips and glue the bottom of the ball to an appropriate sized piece of card. It is now ready to be decorated and turned into a fantasy style bauble. Choose a colour scheme for your bauble and collect a range of different sorts of paper that fit it e.g. a warm colour scheme might include gold foil, yellow, orange and red papers plus some art straws as additional decoration. If there are papers resulting from marbling, colour mixing, printing etc. in previous sessions, that match your colour scheme then use these as well. Start with a sheet of coloured tissue paper and gently stuff this inside your ball structure, it will need to be 'tweaked' in places to keep a ball like shape even though it is on the inside. Use a range of papers, paper shapes (strips, circles etc.) and paper skills (curls, fringes etc.) to add decoration to the outside of the bauble. Think of a special type of decoration to put on the top to make it stand out, also add decoration to the base on which the bauble stands - this will need to go round or radiate from the bauble shape itself. These fantasy baubles could be displayed on a flat surface with a basket of actual baubles - or they could be attached to the wall by their bases.

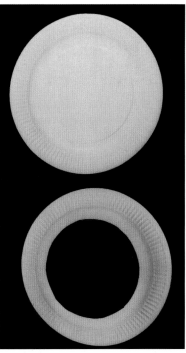

7. *Paper Plate Baubles*

8. *Paper Strip Fantasy Baubles*

9. Torn Paper Plaques

Materials Needed: Paper plates (large), assorted coloured plain papers, foil, tissue paper, glue, scissors, pencils, pre-cut paper circles and stars - for central motifs, (older children could design and cut out their own central motifs).

What to do: Decide on a colour family for your plaque i.e. different shades of one colour, and collect a range of papers in your colour choice. Choose one of these papers to cover the centre of your plate, lay the plate on it, draw round it, cut the drawn circle out and glue it on to your plate. Decide on a central motif for your plate and cut it out of a different paper in your colour collection and stick it in the centre of the covered plate. Add extra decoration to it if you wish e.g. strips, scrunched tissue paper balls etc. Tear strips of paper (long and short) from all the other papers you have collected and glue them around the edge of your plate. Allow them to overlap, curl over and stick out beyond the edge of the plate like a starburst.

10. Cut and Fold Paper Plaques

Materials Needed: Paper plates (large) plus assorted papers as above, maths shapes of various sizes to draw round, ready mixed paint, pieces of card as palettes, sponge rollers, and cotton wool buds for printing.

What to do: As above decide on a colour family for your plaque i.e. different shades of one colour and collect a range of papers in your colour choice. Decide whether you want to keep your plate white or colour it in a shade of your chosen colour family. If you are going to colour it, mix the paint and use a sponge roller to apply it to the surface of the plate. An uneven colour mix can look effective. Draw round some of the maths shapes on the different papers you have collected, cut them out and explore ways of folding them and cutting them to make new shapes e.g. 1/2 circles and shapes that stand up e.g. cones, rolls etc. Arrange these shapes to make a pattern on your plate, start with a central design, then add a repeat pattern around the edge. Add further interest with a little printing and arranging smaller shapes on top of the larger ones.

11. Black and White Doors

Materials Needed: Pieces of white card approx 30 x 30 cm, black sugar paper, art straws, scissors, glue, pencils, rulers, pictures of different styles of doors for ideas.

What to Do: Measure 8cm in at the top and bottom of one edge of the card. Use a ruler and a closed pair of scissors to score a line joining these measurements. Fold the piece of card backwards along the scored line. On the same edge now measure 3cm in at the top and bottom and use a ruler and scissors to score a line joining these measurements. This time fold the card forwards along the scored line. Repeat the same on the opposite parallel edge of the card. This should give you a raised central panel that will become the door, a folded strip that pushes this panel forward, and two narrower strips to attach the finished door to the wall for display, or to make it more stable if it is to be free standing. Look at different door designs, panels, fanlights, door furniture etc. to help with designing your door. Cut and arrange the shapes you decide on out of black paper and art straws and attach them to the front panel of your card to create the door - remember gaps are important in the design as well as the shapes. Display the doors in a row next to each other. Creative writing about the families behind the doors could be added or envelopes addressed to them as if Christmas cards were being delivered. In addition a row of cut-out black foot prints could be placed below the doors and possibly even holly wreaths fastened to some of them.

9. Torn Paper Plaques

10. Cut and Fold Paper Plaques

11. Black and White Doors

Other titles in the series include:

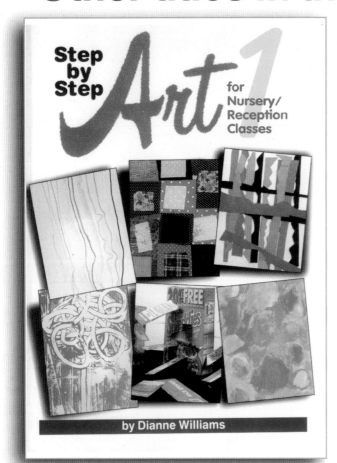

Step by Step Art **1** for Nursery/Reception Classes
by Dianne Williams

Step by Step Art **2** for Key Stage 1 Classes
by Dianne Williams

Step by Step Art **3** for Lower Key Stage 2 Classes
by Dianne Williams

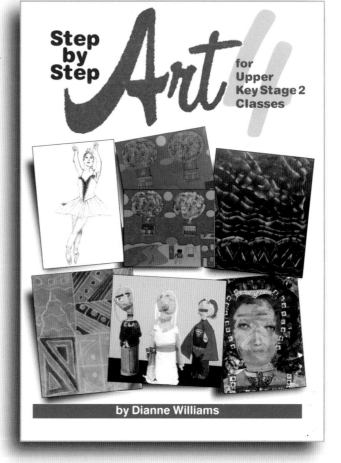

Step by Step Art **4** for Upper Key Stage 2 Classes
by Dianne Williams